A LADYBIRD

H R H CATHERINE

THE *D*UCHESS OF CAMBRIDGE

AN ORDINARY GIRL IS BORN

Catherine Elizabeth Middleton (known as Kate) was born on 9 January 1982, the eldest of three children. Even though Kate was given the middle name Elizabeth,

Kate's parents, Michael and Carole

Michael and Carole Middleton might have believed that any connection to the Queen would end there. The Middleton family is very far from royalty, for whilst The Duke of Cambridge's grandmother is Queen, Kate's grandmother was a humble shop assistant.

The Middletons' home in Berkshire

When Kate was only two years old, her father's work in the airline industry took the young family, including Kate's new sister, Philippa (Pippa), to Amman in Jordan, where they settled happily for over two years. At a nursery school in Amman, Kate learned to sing 'Happy Birthday' in Arabic before she could sing the song in English!

Kate Middleton as a child

SCHOOL LIFE

In September 1986, Kate and her family returned to the United Kingdom and in 1987 her little brother, James, was born. The family settled in the picturesque village of Bucklebury in Berkshire.

For the next nine years, Kate attended St Andrew's School in Pangbourne, near her family home. For much of this time, Prince William was at school at Ludgrove, less than 15 miles away. He even visited St Andrew's once, aged ten, to play a hockey match, although the two never met.

At St Andrew's, Kate (front, centre) enjoyed a lot of different sports

Prince William plays tennis at Ludgrove

Kate went on to Marlborough College in Wiltshire, where she studied Chemistry, Biology and Art at A-level. She also excelled at school sports, playing tennis, hockey, netball and taking part in athletics.

Marlborough College

UNIVERSITY YEARS

St Salvator's Hall, University of St Andrews, Fife, Scotland

After taking a gap year, Kate began her degree course at the University of St Andrews, Scotland, in 2001. Her chosen subject was History of Art, and she soon became known as 'the prettiest girl' at St Salvator's Hall of residence.

Prince William was taking the same degree course so they met often, with the future king commenting that early on he 'knew there was something very special about her'.

In their second year, Kate and William moved into a flat with mutual friends and their friendship slowly turned to romance.

Kate and William quickly became good friends

A happy Kate and William on their graduation day in 2005

Kate at her graduation ceremony

Kate and Prince William both graduated from St Andrews in 2005. Kate then started work for the clothing firm Jigsaw as an accessories buyer, as well as helping out at her parents' party planning company.

A ROYAL ENGAGEMENT

The young couple tried hard to conduct their relationship privately. Eventually, to everyone's delight, Prince William proposed during a holiday to Kenya in October 2010. He presented Kate with the sapphire and diamond engagement ring his father had given his mother, Diana, almost thirty years before.

William and Kate make a glamorous couple

When the engagement was officially announced on 16 November 2010, Kate gave her first media interview, sounding a little nervous but looking very happy!

Over the following months, huge excitement surrounded the eagerly awaited royal wedding. The world speculated on the design of the dress, the wording of the vows and who would be on the guest list.

The happy couple pose for photographers at St James's Palace, London

THE WEDDING

Westminster Abbey, London

At last the big day arrived! On 29 April 2011, wedding fever gripped the nation. Towns and streets were decorated with bunting and flags, and crowds celebrated everywhere.

As Kate slowly made her way into Westminster Abbey, the world gasped. The bride wore a gown of ivory and white satin gazar, with an ivory satin bodice complete with 58 covered buttons and a train almost 3 metres long. The Queen had loaned Kate a magnificent tiara to wear and the bride's parents had given her a beautiful pair of diamond earrings as a wedding gift.

The arrival of the bride with her maid of honour, sister Pippa

The married couple leave the abbey to cheers from the crowds

The wedding party

Upon their marriage, the Queen bestowed upon the newlyweds the titles of The Duke and Duchess of Cambridge.

The Duke and Duchess make their way down the Mall to Buckingham Palace

Although the royal bride must have felt nervous, she appeared calm and composed. This cannot have been easy with 1,900 guests in Westminster Abbey itself and a worldwide television audience of millions of people watching her every move.

After the ceremony, The Duke and Duchess of Cambridge began the short journey back to Buckingham Palace in a traditional landau (horse-drawn carriage). They passed huge crowds of well-wishers, many of whom had camped out for days in the hope of glimpsing the royal newlyweds.

No royal wedding is complete without a balcony appearance at Buckingham Palace. As soon as the Royal Family stepped outside, waving and smiling, thousands of cheers could be heard and flags were waved in celebration.

The fairy tale wedding captured the hearts of people all around the world

William and Catherine kiss on the balcony

MARRIED LIFE

William is a search and rescue helicopter pilot

William and Catherine spent their honeymoon on a secluded Seychelles island before returning to their quiet country life in Anglesey, North Wales. The couple had been living there in order to be close to William's job with the RAF. Whether at home in Wales or in London, William and Catherine are keen to keep their lives as ordinary as possible.

The Duchess of Cambridge shopping on the Kings Road, London

Some months after their wedding, the royal newlyweds proudly welcomed a new addition to their family – a black cocker spaniel puppy named Lupo! He is good company for Catherine when William is away, and she enjoys the freedom and privacy that long walks around her secluded home afford her.

Catherine and Lupo watch Prince William and Prince Harry at a polo match in Gloucestershire in 2012

A ROYAL ROLE

Catherine gave her first public speech in March 2012

After their marriage, William and Catherine were keen to return to their royal duties. In the time since Kate Middleton became Her Royal Highness The Duchess of Cambridge, she has gradually begun to take on more royal duties, even carrying out a few solo engagements.

Catherine enjoys her royal duties

Catherine supports her husband in his charitable work and, in January 2012, the Duchess became patron of four charities of her own: The Art Room, the National Portrait Gallery in London, Action on Addiction and East Anglia's Children's Hospices, all of which were chosen carefully by the Duchess herself. She has also become a volunteer member of The Scout Association and will join them on their adventures when time allows!

Catherine meets some young members of The Scout Association

Within three months of their marriage, the Duke and Duchess went on their first overseas tour as a married couple. They spent eleven days in Canada and the United States of America, where William and Catherine were met by cheering crowds wherever they went.

Catherine and William on their first royal tour together

In the summer of 2012, the Duke and Duchess took a nine-day tour of South East Asia and the South Pacific to celebrate the Queen's Diamond Jubilee. At the Singapore Botanic Gardens, the royal couple saw a species of orchid named after William's mother, Diana, Princess of Wales.

William and Catherine on their royal tour of Asia

FIRST MILESTONES

Catherine spent her first Christmas as part of the Royal Family in 2011, at Sandringham House in Norfolk. Next, in June 2012, the Duchess played her part in commemorating the Queen's Diamond Jubilee.

Catherine joins the family as they walk from Sandringham House to the church on Christmas Day

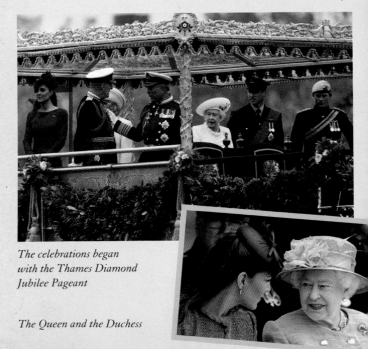

The celebrations began with the Thames Diamond Jubilee Pageant

The Queen and the Duchess

Later in the same year, along with her husband, Catherine was an official ambassador for Team GB and Paralympics GB during the Olympic and Paralympic Games in London. She was often seen supporting the competitors and helped cheer on Zara Phillips, the Duke's cousin, to a silver medal in the equestrian team event. The Duchess seemed as excited as anyone to be part of these enormous worldwide celebrations.

Zara Phillips celebrates her silver medal win

William and Catherine celebrate Great Britain's Olympic success

GREAT BRITAIN

TEAM GB

QUEEN OF FASHION

The Duke and Duchess meet the President of the United States and his wife

Catherine's style is classic and elegant. The Duchess knows what clothes suit her and likes to stick to simple, well-cut designs.

Catherine loves to wear beautiful designer gowns, but she is also a fan of high street fashion. The dress she wore to meet President Obama and his wife, Michelle, was from the high street store Reiss, which sold out of the dress within hours of Catherine wearing it!

Catherine wearing stunning dresses by designers Roksanda Ilincic (left) and Jenny Packham (abov

Catherine wore a red hat decorated with maple leaves during the royal tour of Canada, and her choice of a white cable-knit Alexander McQueen dress for Wimbledon was perfect. Catherine is confident in her fashion choices, and she is not afraid to wear something more than once.

The Duchess is a staunch supporter of British designers

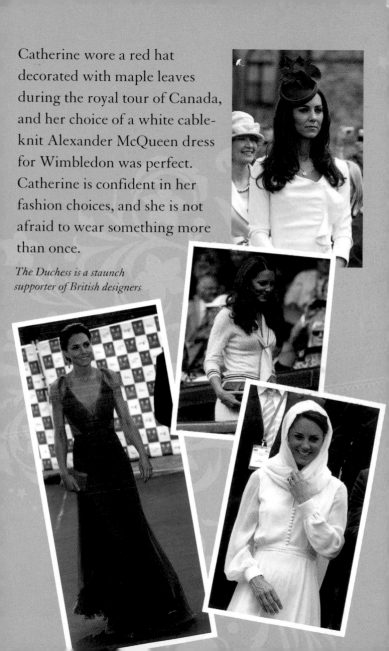

THE FUTURE

The Duchess visits Alder Hey Children's Hospital in Liverpool

The Royal Family is changing and, in 2012, Commonwealth leaders agreed to change succession laws. This means the sons and daughters of any future monarch will have equal right to the throne. If William and Catherine's first child is a baby girl she will one day become Queen, and any younger brothers will not take precedence. Now that the Duke and Duchess will be starting a family of their own, Catherine will find herself with yet another role to play: that of mother to a future king or queen.

A visit to Rose Hill Primary School in Oxford has all the children cheering

Catherine meets children in Newcastle upon Tyne, as she visits a community garden

The day that Kate Middleton married a prince and became Her Royal Highness Catherine The Duchess of Cambridge, her life changed forever. The eyes of the world are watching as she takes each confident step towards the next stage of her life as an important member of the British Royal Family.